The True Story of
Surviving a Fallen Trooper

ONE
DARK
MORNING

LINDA Q. CAVAZOS

One Dark Morning

The True Story of
Surviving a Fallen Trooper

Linda Q. Cavazos

SB
Sigma Books

© 2020 Linda Q. Cavazos. All Rights Reserved.
ISBN: 978-1-67801-086-7
Published by Sigma Books

To my daughter and son

Contents

1

One Dark Morning

I did not hear the shots.

I was not at the horrific murder scene.

Instead in the early morning hours of a cold February 24, 1993, I was home in bed, peacefully asleep. It was the last peaceful sleep I would have for months.

I learned later from an eyewitness's testimony at the trial that the shots sounded like *Pow-Pow.*

As this first witness came around the bend of the exit ramp off I-95, Virginia State Police Trooper José Cavazos was falling forward onto the roadway.

The coroner's report documented that my husband's face was scratched from the impact and his reading glasses were smashed.

Two of the six bullet wounds to José's body were fatal. Two Black Talon bullets entered on either side of the collarbone above the protective vest he wore.

The coroner said that José probably died within minutes as he bled to death. He was not able to move from where he fell on the roadway.

My daughter asked if her father had time to think before he died, and if he did, would his thoughts have been about his family. Did he suffer? Was his pain unbearable?

I wish I had been there to hold his hand, to say farewell.

I had an empty feeling because there was no warning for us. In the blink of an eye he disappeared from our world.

2

My World

I grew up on an isolated cattle farm in the Piedmont region of Virginia at the foot of the Blue Ridge Mountains.

Greenville Farm was a 388-acre spread located near Raccoon Ford in Culpeper County. And for twenty years, that was my world.

But my family's roots go back to Cherokee, North Carolina.

Born in 1847, my great grandfather the Reverend William Haynes Queen was a Baptist minister and farmer in Cherokee. Some years ago, I visited the small, white church where William preached, and I wondered how many parishioners attended his services. Was he charismatic?

In 1878, he married Sarah Ann Fisher. She was to take part in the great family migration north to Virginia. But I'm getting ahead of myself.

In 1910, William attended the wedding of his son Thomas "Cling" Clingman Queen and Miriam Margaret Miller, my grandparents.

Then everything changed in Cherokee.

In 1933, the Queens were required to sell their North Carolina land. Why? The federal government was developing a new national park: Great Smoky Mountains National Park.

Along with the Parker family, Cling and Miriam Queen came to Virginia and purchased Greenville Farm.

They were accompanied by his mother Sarah and their

seven children, including their son Vernon, my future father, who was sixteen at the time.

The large home on the farm was a Classical Revival structure. Built in the mid-1800s, the red brick, three-story house was dominated by four 30-foot Tuscan columns.

Cling and Miriam moved into it immediately upon leaving North Carolina. And they lived there until their death.

This grandiose building was unique. The home was set on an English basement, much like a townhouse. It was three floors, 54 x 38 feet, with a low-pitched roof.

The home had two entrances. The front entrance had a wooden landing and was accessed between the columns. It led into a central hall. The rear entrance led into the basement and upstairs to the ground floor, which had a back porch with a shed roof.

There were three interior chimneys. One chimney was on the east wall, with two chimneys on the west.

Originally, the basement level was for dining and the ground level for entertaining, while the top level had bed chambers.

The main stairway occupied the center of the home. The historic record states that an open-well, circular stair with a walnut wood railing "ascends to the top floor." The stairway began in the basement and had a turned newel, a rounded handrail, and square balusters, two to a tread.

This was one of few great country homes built before the Civil War. It is similar to homes built in the Deep South rather than those built in central Virginia at the time.

Philip Pendleton Nalle, whose ancestors had lived in Culpeper since the mid-1700s, operated a mercantile establishment at Raccoon Ford. It was probably this source of income that paved the way to his purchasing Greenville Farm.

In 1847, he purchased the land from a man named Thomas Wharton for $9,700.
However, during the home's construction in 1852, the country was in an economic downturn. His improvements of the new home on the Greenville tract were listed at $4,000. Tax records show he had a hundred head of cattle as my father later did when he ran the farm.

During the Civil War, the massive home lay between Union and Confederate lines. In one battle, Confederate forces were positioned on a hill overlooking the home from the south side of the Rapidan River, while the Union lines split through the middle of the property. Historical records describe how bullets whistled back and forth and residents were afraid to go outside.

A field next to the yard area was later called "cannonball field." Sometimes when plowing the fields, my grandfather and father would find miniature balls along with arrowheads.

The home supposedly served as a hospital for the wounded during the Civil War, and rumors held that there was an escape tunnel from the home to the river. My father and his siblings searched for the tunnel numerous times, but never found it.

In 1905 upon Nalle's death, the home was passed to his son, Philip Pendleton Nalle, Jr.

In 1933 when my family bought the land and structures thereon, like many farms during the Great Depression it was in foreclosure.

But the Queen family had arrived. And Greenville Farm was our world for three generations.

When my parents married in 1941, they resided in the home for a year.

Then my father built a second home on the land for his growing family. I grew up in a modern house with all the modern conveniences of the 1950s. But my grandparents' house remained the center of family gatherings.

When I was a child, the winters were icy cold. Whenever we visited, I would run up the circular stairs to the top level where we grandchildren slept. It was the only heated bedroom, heated by a wood stove and not very warm. Once in bed, I shivered under the covers. The big, homemade featherbeds were absolutely necessary.

I remember the extended Parker family living in the English basement with a private kitchen. My grandparents Cling and Miriam built their own kitchen on the ground level. Later when running water was installed, the only bathroom in the home was on that level.

Miriam was a master at heat control of the wood stove in her kitchen. What a skill to stoke that fire with just the correct amount of wood. I can still see the flames when she opened the lid to the stove cavity.

I remember the aroma of "Grand Mom's" southern breakfasts, with bacon or ham from farm hogs, eggs, and biscuits with white gravy. Once in a while I was allowed to savor a sip of coffee. It was the strongest coffee I have ever tasted.

For the holidays, Miriam often baked her fantastic homemade cinnamon buns, which always rose to perfection. The buns were garnished with raisins and white sugar glaze.

Each day, the three meals she cooked included biscuits or cornbread, each made without measurement; she just added a handful of this or that.

Besides being an exceptional cook, she worked hard raising a large family, sewing clothes, gardening, and cleaning. She planted a huge vegetable garden every year and canned on the hottest days of summer. She also fed crews when they came to the farm to help with harvests.

I grew up in a safe, loving, sheltered environment.

News came to my farm by way of the *Washington Post* newspaper or on a radio where the newsman broadcast over an airway interrupted by static.

When we were teenagers, our news sometimes came to us on the telephone party line, which our household shared with four other families. If one picked up the receiver slowly, those in conversation might not know that someone was "listening in."

Since my nearest friend was thirteen miles away, I was lonely sometimes and very lonely many times.

My bus ride to school was about forty-five minutes. Just the road from my house to the bus pick-up point was a mile. My mom drove us to the bus each morning and picked us up each afternoon.

Since news traveled slowly, when a massive snowstorm started one day and school was released early, our parents didn't know. My sister and I walked home against cold winds, sleet, and blinding visibility. At times, we knew we were lost, but at last we made it home.

We ice-skated on the farm pond and on the creek that was in the front section of the land. I remember my feet feeling frozen from such cold adventures as my socks were pathetically thin.

My dad built our home on the "hill" overlooking the antebellum main home on Greenville Farm. He installed central heat because he said he had spent too much of his childhood cutting wood and carrying it inside to heat his family's large home. He built much of the house with the help of a neighbor. It was small, but comfortable.

The sunsets were gorgeous. Five sugar maples framed the north and west side of our yard. Their leaves turned yellow in the fall.

We were surrounded by manicured pasture in the front and corn or grain crops in the back fields, with the barns a quarter mile away. The Rapidan River bordered the rear of our property, separating our farm in Culpeper County from Orange County to the south.

My dad, who was always busy, got up early in both the winter and summer. Several times in the spring and summer, he mowed the fields, assuring an immaculate, beautiful property.

But life was not as idyllic for me as it might have appeared. I was overshadowed by my sister Elsa, always feeling not as smart, less favored, less goal-oriented, and often slighted because I didn't have as many dates as she.

But isn't it common in families that the first-born rules? I belittled myself, but finally discovered I was also smart and sociable.

I was in the gifted program by eighth grade. And I had brown eyes and blonde hair, which was a rare combination. Pictures from teen years and early twenties reveal a pretty girl.

I laughed a lot and was told as a small child that I never sat down; I ran instead of walked. I was gregarious when it was necessary in order to have friends and be "popular."

But deep inside, I was shy.

I graduated high school after completing the advanced studies curriculum. I did well on the SATs and was accepted to the College of William & Mary in Williamsburg.

I completed two years at W&M, but struggled to find my path in college. I couldn't decide my major or figure out what field was best for me.

So I returned to live at home and search for work. My first job after leaving college was with the Federal Bureau of Investigation.

The FBI was recruiting young men and women. I answered a newspaper ad and met the recruitment officer in Fredericksburg, Virginia for an interview.

Special Agent Brennan was jovial and known for hiring good-looking females. I must have satisfied his requirements and, just as importantly, passed a background check.

Many recruits were tagged to work in Washington, DC at the fingerprint lab, but I wanted to work closer to home. So I chose to work in Richmond, the capital of the commonwealth.

In 1965, I left my home on the farm and moved to Richmond, where my job with the FBI began.

The FBI Director at the time was J. Edgar Hoover. All new hires were required to meet Mr. Hoover, so I traveled to headquarters in Washington, DC to meet him.

After our group entered the room in single file, photographs were taken with Mr. Hoover in the middle. I wore a grey mini dress and white gloves and small heels. My hair was teased and very blonde that day. I presented myself with confidence, but had no agenda to stand out among the women. I wasn't the type of woman who dressed provocatively.

It was the mid-1960s, and our caseload at work involved large national issues, including deserters who shirked service in the Vietnam War.

I was young and naïve and didn't understand the importance of changes that were happening in the USA. President Kennedy had been assassinated in 1963. North Korea captured the *USS Pueblo* on January 23, 1968. The Tet Offensive in Vietnam began seven days later. Martin Luther King, Jr. was killed on April 4, 1968. JFK's brother Bobby Kennedy was killed by gunfire exactly two months later. Neil Armstrong and Buzz Aldrin walked on the Moon on July 21, 1969 (I still remember where I watched that on television). We had riots against the war, and four students were shot to death by National Guardsmen on March 4, 1970 at Kent State University.

Blacks felt discrimination, but so did women. At the FBI, women weren't accepted to work as special agents. We were the stenographic and clerical side of the operation. The sexual revolution was beginning, yet when I bought my first home in the early 1970s, I was asked to prove I was on birth control pills before the loan was approved, because my salary helped get the loan. I remember being offended and angry over that, which was in my opinion an irrelevant intrusion into my life.

Distribution of The Ten Most Wanted list was another part of my duties. The list sometimes included black militants, such as members of the Black Panthers. The civil rights movement was gaining force. Patty Hearst was a criminal on the Most Wanted list after she was kidnapped in 1974, when she was 20, by the Symbionese Liberation Army.

I worked for the FBI for half a decade. It was a busy and difficult job, and my world was expanding.

In 1982, after I had grown up, gotten a job, and moved away, my family finally left Greenville Farm.

I was happy that the new owners, Bill and Adrianne Foshay, were intent on continuing to farm the nearly 400 acres. But fifteen years after buying the land, they also decided to restore the antebellum home.

Because the building had been vacant for some years, it was in disrepair. Before restoring it in 1998, the Foshays said they could look up through the house to the top level while standing in the basement.

Now it stands as proud as ever, a lasting memory of the world in which I grew up.

The restored Greenville Home
Raccoon Ford, Virginia (2016)

3

Devastation

I could not believe the doorbell's chime so early in the morning. It was around 12:30 a.m., February 24th. It was Ash Wednesday. Who in the world was it?

I was groggy, didn't even grab a robe. I put on an old pair of glasses with one broken lens, and with minimal fear, I opened the front door.

Outside on the stoop was a sergeant from my husband's barracks in Independent Hill, Virginia.

He told me my husband José had an accident and I needed to come with him.

My daughter was living at college in Charlottesville, but my son was sixteen and asleep in his bedroom. I asked if he should come.

Yes, he said. He should come, too.

The sergeant took the wheel and we sped away toward Washington Hospital Center, north of the U.S. Capitol in Washington, DC. We flew past cars, never yielding, because the police made a path for us. But I didn't realize it at the time.

My son talked about how smart Dad was and that he would be fine no matter what.

I prayed to myself, "Do not let José be paralyzed. He would be miserable to lose mobility."

I was scared, and focused my thoughts on my husband's smile and possible wounds inflicted on his face. He was a handsome, attractive man. I prayed for his face to be spared from injury. He had the greatest smile, and thick and wavy salt-and-pepper hair which, combined with his 6'1" frame, made him distinguished. He always took my breath away.

My son and I arrived and were escorted into a small room.

I didn't think about death. Instead, I hoped big time for minor injuries. We remained alone for about twenty minutes.

Finally, the door opened and a number of people stormed in. I remember seeing some white medical coats. Everyone seemed to be rushing. No one took time to identify themselves. It was as though a quarterback passed me a football, and I dared not miss the catch.

One of the bearers of the nightmare news, I don't remember if male or female, said to me and my son, "Your husband did not live."

After this announcement, my body fell onto the floor.

Leaning over me was the Colonel of the State Police.

In the background, I heard my son speak in a shocked tone. He was a kid, not a man, and needed a dad. He blurted out exclamations to everyone in the room, and he was angry.

When we left that dreadful room, I was in a wheelchair, and my son walked beside me.

The police had notified my sister and brother-in-law, and they took us home.

I said, "They have shot and killed him!"

And finally I cried.

I did not see my husband's body at the hospital; I never asked to see him. I had lost all reasoning, I suppose, and I just did what I was told. That was a mistake on my part and I should have said good-bye to him by touching him. He would have done that for me.

Someone on the medical staff gave me a prescription for sleeping pills and suggested I go home and sleep. It was a thoughtful, caring, fairly routine act, but showed the hospital personnel didn't understand what death does to survivors. It was not unkind to be told to go home and sleep; it simply lacked understanding.

Not one person, except my sister, said they were sorry, No one but my son felt my pain. I experienced a daunting, hopeless moment.

My hopelessness endured for weeks.

LINDA Q. CAVAZOS

4

A Love Story

I was married when I was twenty-three, on March 22, 1969. I fell in love with José Cavazos, who had recently moved to Richmond, Virginia from Edinburg, Texas.

We attended a dance on our first date after meeting at the home of my friend Sandy Broaddus who wanted us to meet. Sandy thought we would be a compatible couple.

I was instantly attracted to him. He was tall and handsome, smart and confident. José told me that evening that he thought I was Sandy's child's babysitter because I looked so young.

We decided quickly to commit to monogamous dating. Once we became engaged, my Episcopalian upbringing dictated a respect for the marriage vows.

I believed I would be married for life and my husband and I would be parted only by death. I anticipated a long and happy life with José.

My Anglo-Saxon background quickly blended superbly with his Mexican-American heritage.

In my twenty-three years, I hadn't met many people who spoke two languages. My limited understanding of the world outside of my rural parameters was a vast contrast to today's world when the Internet offers information in a flash. Many countries in today's world are tethered by social media and instantaneous Google searches.

I relish the fact that I didn't think it a bad decision to get engaged to José, or that I wasn't aware that I might suffer backlash to marry out of my ethnicity.

But the Episcopal priest who gave us premarital sessions warned us our marriage wouldn't last because our backgrounds were too different. We were doomed, he said, because of our differences. Not just because José was Catholic, but because he was Mexican.

I didn't believe the minister's negative warnings, and he didn't intimidate me. Nor did I consider changing my mind about this fantastic love I had found.

I didn't know that in some states we wouldn't have been able to marry at all. Once I fell in love with José, I accepted him as a human being, viewed him as the smart man that he was, rather than someone inferior to me.

We had known each other for six months before our wedding day.

Our wedding was held in St. Bartholomew's, a modern yet unadorned mission church. The plain surroundings did not diminish the event, and my innermost thoughts were melodic, as though I were feeling the beat of a vibrant poem. I created my own Biblical, stained glass images in my mind and envisioned a beautiful storybook romance for José and me, and thought we would love until old age. Luckily, I could not foresee our future.

Our wedding day was a sunny, beautiful day. Forsythia was blooming, one of the first flowers of spring in Virginia. I was nervous because I feared José wouldn't show up at the ceremony. I don't know why I was fearful, but I breathed a big sigh once I saw him walk up the path in the rear of the church to meet the minister.

Mr. and Mrs. José Cavazos
March 22, 1969. Richmond, Virginia

My gown was white silk organza and Chantilly lace, an Empire-style dress, floor length, and ever so dainty. The dress emphasized my slim, tall figure. My borrowed, full-length veil fell from a pillbox hat, and I carried my white Episcopalian prayer book adorned with a butterfly orchid, white stephanotis flowers, and a cascade of ribbons.

Brides in the 1960s usually wore white gloves, and I remember cutting the seam of the left ring finger on the glove, so my finger was ready for my wedding ring.

José was in a dark grey tuxedo with tails. I came down the aisle on my father's arm, and I was thinking, "Well yes, I will definitely take this man to be my wedded husband!"

I felt very confident. I was uplifted and so in love.

We were a handsome couple decked out in our traditional wedding garb, very much in style for a 1960s wedding. Our love was evident in our smiles, in our warm embraces, and our family and friends must have sensed our happiness.

A lively reception followed at my sister's house. The dining table was adorned by a tiered cake, non-alcoholic punch, mints, and nuts. Traditional Southern wedding receptions most often didn't require a seated dinner reception, unless the couple lived above the Mason-Dixon Line.

I left for the honeymoon in a grey sheath dress matched with a grey checked jacket. My purse, hat, and heels were pink.

We were showered with rice as we ran to our "getaway car." Of course, rice is no longer allowed at weddings. My co-workers also stuffed my suitcase full of the white dots generated from the National Crime Information Center computer data cards at my office. Yes, computers were appearing. It seems so long ago.

In the book of Genesis, the purpose of a man and woman's union is explained:

"God shaped man from the dust of the ground and breathed into his nostrils the breath of life; and man became a living soul.

"And the Lord God planted a Garden eastward in Eden; and there he put the man he had formed." (Genesis 2:7-8)

"And the rib, which the Lord God had taken from the man, made he a woman, and brought her unto the man." (Genesis 2:22)

"Therefore shall a man leave his father and his mother and shall cleave unto his wife and they shall be one flesh." (Genesis 2:24)

Adam was lonely, and God knew that he was lonely and created woman, a partner and helper and someone with whom to bear children. Eve rose from Adam's rib.

I believe it was God's plan that José and I were destined to meet at a time and place we could never have predicted. José and I were both searching for a spouse. We were well into our twenties and ready to be a couple.

Besides, I felt an instant spark that burnt my face, burnt my skin. It was an unstoppable attraction I felt towards this handsome young man whom I was eager to accept as my husband.

5

José Maria Cavazos

José was born and raised in Edinburg, Texas, twenty miles from the Mexican border.

His entire family was of Mexican descent.

José's grandfather, named Eligio Benavides Cavazos, was born in Reynosa, Mexico tucked in the northeast corner of the country, on the southern bank of the Rio Grande.

Eligio married Adeladia Dominquez in 1863. His second wife was named Juana Navarro. As a result, Eligio had two sets of children.

The older siblings didn't know that their younger half-siblings existed.

In this second family, there were three sons and a younger sister, Guadalupe. But their mother died in childbirth, and Guadalupe was sent to live with her god-mother.

The middle son Manuel was born in Reynosa in 1900. It was a prosperous time in Mexico, and the country was nearing the end of a thirty-year period of political stability and economic growth.

The Cavazos family owned land in northern Mexico. But Eligio and Pancho Villa were enemies. He was afraid his children's lives were in peril, so he decided to send them away from Mexico.

The three sons went to live with Amada Barrera, their maternal grandmother and a mother of nine who lived in the United States.

I remember José talking about his Mexican ancestry and the several revolutions that plagued Mexico and his family between 1910-1920. I wish I had listened more attentively.

The family apparently lost its land holdings during the uprisings, which were waged against the wealthy.

I wish there was more documentation of the plight of the family, but I imagine life was very unstable and stressful.

Manuel Cavazos was about thirteen when he was separated from his family in Mexico and went to live twenty-five miles due north in Edinburg, Texas.

Eleven years later on October 31, 1924, he married Jesusa Aguirre, also of Mexican ancestry. But she was an American citizen, born just up the Rio Grande Valley in Roma, Texas.

Together, they produced three daughters and five sons. The last son was José Maria Cavazos, born at home on Christmas Day, 1942.

Life wasn't easy for the growing Cavazos family. Manuel and Jesusa were migrant workers in the United States. They and their children traveled frequently during the harvest seasons.

By the time José was born, his dad was a cowboy on a ranch, so young José didn't travel much as a migrant child.

Restaurants in some states didn't serve Mexicans in the 1940s. Prejudice was dominant. So when his family did travel as migrants, José had a special job. He was blond-haired at age five and, looking Caucasian, would go into restaurants to buy food for the family.

Migrant workers' children missed months of school, but the Cavazos children played "catch up" well.

One brother became a CPA. The oldest son enlisted in the army at seventeen and served over twenty years. Another brother became a high school principle and superintendent. And José's oldest sister earned a teaching degree after she had six children.

They were a poor family, but I am confident their parents urged them to study and strive for success.

José learned both English and Spanish in the public schools and was a good student. His siblings told me he was smarter than his grades reflected.

José attended the University of Texas–Pan American in Edinburg, Texas and earned two years of college credits.

At twenty-two, he also joined the National Guard. In the fall of 1964, he completed basic training at Fort Polk, Louisiana with the Army's National Guard training program. He was in the National Guard for six years.

He told me a brief story about his deciding to leave Texas at twenty-six. It was 1968, and he had been turned down for a highway patrol position in Texas because the state didn't hire Hispanics as policemen. He packed a few belongings in a small suitcase, put on jeans and a jeans jacket, bought a ticket on a Greyhound bus, and traveled 2200 miles on that bus.

He wasn't afraid to leave his home in South Texas, because he was angry. He believed his life would be better on the East Coast of the United States. His bus traveled through the huge expanse of Texas, east into Arkansas, the entire length of Tennessee, and finally into the beautiful roads that led to his destination, Richmond, Virginia.

José went to work for the telephone company in Virginia soon upon arriving in that Southern state. Two of his friends from Edinburg were living in Richmond and encouraged him to settle there permanently.

Soon he met Paige Schultz, who was the best man at our wedding and worked with José as a lineman.

José was climbing poles in the worst of weather and working to restore phone service in winter. He moved from a warm climate in Texas to Virginia that had its share of harsh winter storms. I remember his stories of climbing poles in sleet and snowstorms in a warm coat given to him by a friend, Feliz Perez.

Later that year he enrolled in Virginia Commonwealth University to continue a degree program, and got a new job with Virginia Motor Vehicles.

In 1981, he joined the Army Reserves in Virginia. A decade later, he was deployed to the Gulf War. Attached to an Army Reserve Unit from Charleston, West Virginia, he served during Desert Storm. He was an interrogator who worked with a translator to question Iraqi prisoners.

He was stationed near the burning oil fields in Kuwait. When he returned from war, he spoke of the smoke clouding the sky and blocking out the sun, making it always appear to be night.

After working for the Virginia Department of Motor Vehicles for fifteen years, he joined the Virginia State Police in 1984, working as a Weight Enforcement Officer.

On July 17, 1986, he graduated from the Virginia State Police Academy. He had the distinction of being the first Mexican-American Virginia State Trooper. At age forty-two, he was also one of the oldest to graduate.

Trooper José M. Cavazos
Graduation photo 1986
Virginia State Police Academy, Richmond, VA

Our children were nine and thirteen at the time, and his classmates called him Poppa. But they assured me he always finished first or second on the mandatory daily run.

As an older trooper, José often reminded new recruits to be careful because there were a lot of crazies on the roads they patrolled. He guided the young troopers to make them aware of the reality on the streets.

Our children and I traveled to Richmond for his graduation. When we left, he drove his police car. I stood and watched him approach his vehicle in his uniform with gun strapped on, and reality hit me. That gun scared me, and finally I realized the danger of his job.

I was naïve, but I wouldn't have changed José's career goals. He knew the dangers of a police officer's work, and I lived each day hoping we would continue to be "lucky."

I was caught up in the daily life of raising a family. And to survive life with a state trooper, I had to ignore the dark, real possibilities.

6

Captured

It took only several hours in the early morning of February 24, 1993 for police officers from Prince William County to apprehend the murderer and the other perpetrator.

The first people to arrive at José's cruiser parked their vehicles behind his and tried to use the radio to call for help, but without luck.

It's ironic that one of the people first on scene during all the confusion witnessed a young black man approach José's body on the ground and pick up something. I learned later during the trial testimony that it was the second killer who picked up his driver's license that had fallen from José's hand.

Eventually, a Lorton Virginia Correctional Officer arrived on scene and was able to summon help over the radio.

People who stopped to help had already covered my husband's body with a thin yellow blanket, as twenty minutes probably had passed since the shooting.

It was February, the road was cold. Later I thought, "What a harsh place to die."

Douglas Buchanan was the first state trooper to arrive at the scene after a radio call announced, "Officer down." He tried cardiopulmonary resuscitation, but José's breath never came back.

I learned later that my husband's lungs had huge gaps when the hollow-point Black Talon bullets, which expand upon entry to target, tore his chest cavity tissues.

When Officer Buchanan turned José over, he had one hand on his gun and one hand under his face.

Police used the canine unit to help in the search. Fairfax County Police Department and the Virginia State Police all assisted in the manhunt.

A twenty-year-old man named Lonnie Weeks, Jr. of Fayetteville, NC and his twenty-one-year old relative Louis Jefferson Dukes, Jr. of Washington, DC were found wandering the parking lot of the Days Inn Motel. I will never understand why they didn't leave the scene. The Days Inn was adjacent to the off ramp of the shooting site. They were soon questioned about the death of Trooper Cavazos.

The two culprits had been traveling in a stolen 1987 Jetta Volkswagen. They had abandoned the vehicle, and later police found the car and a handgun, a 9mm Glock, inside. It was the gun used in the murder.

Why is it that in a brief moment, with no regard for a life, a young man decided to shoot my husband? In seconds, the lives of Lonnie Weeks and Louis Dukes were on an irreversible path to self-destruction. It was such an unreasonable act to be carried out in the darkness of an early morning.

The felons were captured quickly and became subject to the legal system of the Commonwealth of Virginia.

As a victim of this murder, I was also in captivity. Because of this one act, I believed I had no freedom of choice about my future. I faced a tumultuous life I didn't want, one overwhelmed with grief and pain. Peace and comfort were inconceivable.

My family's normalcy was shattered. It took years for

me to recapture who I was. But early on, I was determined to be strong because I didn't want to become mentally unstable.

As I started fighting for myself, I was slowly becoming different. I was becoming a new person to both those I knew and to the public I didn't know at all.

I came home from the hospital and sat at my kitchen table wrapped in a blanket, waiting for word on the criminal investigation.

When I learned of the arrest of two men, I felt no emotion. My mind was stone cold by then, and my brain and heart were in deep pain. I was in shock.

Just like a zombie in that old sci-fi movie, my face was grimaced and my body rigid.

My best friend from high school drove to my home to be with me. I hadn't seen her in years.

A vestryman from my church came by. I still remember Ed and his kindness. He had a cross etched on his forehead made from ashes of palms.

I was captive to the ringing phone, captive to the funeral arrangements facing me.

There were numerous decisions to make. Pallbearers–who would they be? And no, my small country church could not accommodate all the anticipated attendees. What other church could we use? Who from José's family would travel from Texas?

A cemetery in Fairfax, Virginia offered a burial plot. José and I hadn't purchased a burial spot; our life was about living and our children. I was pleased when my uncle offered a plot in the Queen family cemetery at Fairview Cemetery in Culpeper, Virginia.

"Would you prefer a military service or a Virginia

State Police service?" Did I want bagpipes? Did we accept flowers? A multi- gun salute and/or taps? Who will read the Bible verses? On and on and on, all these things to decide, and I was still that zombie.

During the jumbled pre-funeral hours, I couldn't look into my children's eyes. I saw their pain, and they saw mine. The unrelenting pain had all three of us captive.

Surely God stood by my children and me that day. We made it through the service at the church and then proceeded to ride in several white limousines provided the family down Route 29 towards Culpeper to the cemetery.

I had chosen my newest dress, a red and cream floral print, and black shoes to wear. My coat was white with black trim. But underneath I had no energy. Perhaps some folks thought my dress too flashy, but I had decided not to dress in black. What I wore that day was one of the few details left for me to decide as I began my new life.

I was speaking from a mouth that was dry from emotions, and I shed no tears. I remember eating a banana as we headed to the cemetery in the limo. Maybe it was ridiculous to eat a banana on the way to the burial site. But I needed energy because I couldn't fathom how to find the fortitude and courage to see the casket at the cemetery.

How could I allow José's body to descend into that cold ground? How could I accept the folded flag from José's coffin and offer my arms to enfold it? Should I smile?

I was still that captured person who had once planned a future of hope and now faced despair.

7

Tribute

This is my commandment, That ye Love one another, as I have loved you. Greater Love hath no man than this, that a man lay down his life for his friends
–John 15:12-13

This scripture highlighted the preface of the program at José's funeral service on February 27, 1993.

As we remembered my husband and prayed, I realized that his life had been lived for others.

Any person who works as a police officer is selfless. He achieved his goal to be a peace officer, a goal denied in Texas.

When he volunteered to go to Desert Storm with a unit from West Virginia, his decision was patriotic and selfless. He felt it was his duty. He was very patriotic, and had a special bond with his country. It is significant that, in spite of his Mexican heritage and the racial discrimination he felt throughout his life, he was proud to serve his country.

The flag at the United States Capitol in Washington, DC flew at half mast in memory of José's life.

The next week, the flag was delivered to my family.

We knew the citizens of Virginia mourned his death. Ultimately, however, I realized most of the grieving would be our children's and mine.

My seventeen-year-old son wrote about his dad in high school:

"The morning of February 24, 1993, I was awakened

early in the morning. I was told my father was shot. Immediately I thought, He's tough, I'll see him soon. I was very confident that my father was alive. But at the hospital the doctors told us different. Today I still remember every moment of that night.... My father was honest, a hard worker, and full of love. I want to be just like him."

José was young but wanted to retire and rest for a bit. I wonder if he sensed his tragic future. I cannot imagine his wanting to die because he loved us and life so much.

José had endless energy, but little personal time between his state police job and his Army Reservist duties. When he did have time off, he was at home with his family and enjoying his woodworking. He even had a talent for designing and building furniture. He also enjoyed barbecuing and inviting neighbors to eat with us. He was never idle.

He lectured our kids and wanted them to live by high standards. When he died, I felt he had given life his best shot. His life was short, but he lived it fully.

As for me, I wondered what I had done to deserve losing him.

After all, he had common sense and plans for the family. He was such a progressive partner, always the organizer. I had to go on, but my route was not clear.

The public tribute to José was overwhelming.

At least 1,500 people attended his funeral service at St. James Episcopal Church in Warrenton, Virginia, which seated only 300. Local colleagues and officers from many states came. People stood in the church aisles, outside in the reception hall beside the church or in the basement, where they listened to the service by loudspeakers or watched it on television.

People stood along the road and on overpasses on Route 29 as the funeral entourage moved towards the cemetery.

It was a blustery day and snow flurries fell as the sun tried to peek out. I felt it was a beautiful day that provided a perfect goodbye to my beloved.

I don't know how many attendees greeted us at our home.

I stood by the dining table and talked about José with others. We laughed, remembering old stories, hugged, and cried. I thanked everyone for attending and thinking of the children and me.

I was exhausted as were the children when at 10 p.m., I told my sister, "I want my house back. I want some sort of peace. Being surrounded by people is not helping me."

I began to take the small steps needed to regain my life, on my terms.

8

Alone

Those who haven't experienced the death of a loved one might wonder why I felt alone.

After all, neighbors rallied, brought food and visited. They sent sympathy cards and called to ask how the children and I were.

The state police were constantly alert to any need the family had. A handful of José's friends cut and stacked firewood for us, several days after he died. That was so thoughtful, but the troopers said at least that kept them busy doing a chore at our home.

Preston Everhart, one of the chaplains of the Virginia State Police, was supportive for a long time. He would rally me usually by phone calls. He asked me once why I thought it was José who was shot and killed.

I had no answer for that question. I didn't have the stamina to begin to think about it. I wanted to blurt out, "Maybe because God wanted him early on, since he was the perfect candidate for heaven."

Reverend Roma Maycock, my minister from St. Stephen's Episcopal Church in Catlett, Virginia, visited me and said José died because the Devil exists on earth. The Devil makes people do terrible deeds, she said. And it was amazing that during the trial testimony, Lonnie Weeks too said the Devil took over him and made him pull the trigger.

I was bombarded with so many reasons for gun violence, so many opinions on crime, so many news broadcasts, suggestions on how to survive, and gluts of photos of my husband on television. But no one could feel as my children and I did because we missed this man so much.

The day José died, my extended family began to arrive at my home. The press kept asking for a statement, and my brother-in-law finally said that those close to my children and me felt helpless.

What we needed to have was José back and that couldn't happen. How simple it would have been to just get him back. I told a friend the day of the funeral, why can't I be attending a different trooper's funeral?

My mother Wilma Wagner Queen was a timid driver and drove her car only in the small town where she lived. But when I needed her, she willed herself to drive fifty miles to come help me.

I could see in her face the morning of José's death that she was heartbroken. She had lost my dad just two years before.

She was German, a city girl from Philadelphia who married a country boy. She developed excellent survival skills after moving to the farm with her new husband in 1941. The three-story, antebellum house they lived in offered few comforts. There was no heat in her bedroom and no bathroom with running water.

Her motherly duties began when my sister was born ten months after the wedding. I was born three years after that. Our family struggled for financial security, but I always felt loved.

Mom stayed with me after the funeral. She answered the phone, wrote thank you notes to all the kind people who sent flowers and cards to us, cooked meals, and generally kept my house functioning.

I just let her have my duties for a while, which was very unlike me. I had always been in charge of the home front.

Then after a few months, my mother returned home.

Years after José's death, I still struggled with the stigma of being alone. But very early in my grief process, I turned within myself to heal.

I didn't reach out to friends or family to speak of my grief. I meditated and talked to myself. I made myself live and made myself get up each day and go to work.

I talked to my children to try to console them. It was the only way I knew how to help them. I really wanted to help, but I was too limited in that process. I wasn't trained to counsel anyone.

I couldn't accept going to social events alone, going to church alone, and I dreaded the weekends because I was emotionally lost. I believed people judged me as not complete, because I no longer had a husband.

Not only did I have to move through the grief process and understand his death, but also I continued to judge myself as less than whole.

Most happily married couples experience comfort by depending on a partner, a soul mate. Partners do complete the other person. We "hold up" and encourage each other. Since I missed my partner so much, I constantly felt like one good push would send me over that final cliff.

I struggled terribly without my partner. I kept reminding myself I was wasting precious time. How many sermons taught me to enjoy each day I lived as though it were my last. But I continued to stumble and waste precious time.

9

Trials and Punishment

Abhor victimhood. Denounce entitlement. Neither are gifts, rather cages to damn the soul. Everyone who has walked this earth is a victim of injustice. Everyone. Most of all do not be too quick to denounce your sufferings. The difficult road you are called to walk may, in fact, be your only path to success.
–Richard Paul Evans, *A Winter Dream*

The first hearing was held several days after the murder.

The Commonwealth's Attorney for Prince William County Paul Ebert believed Weeks opened fire on José because he was traveling in a stolen car and was violating probation for a drug charge in North Carolina. Weeks panicked when José pulled Dukes behind the vehicle to frisk him. Weeks stepped out of the passenger side and opened fire.

Ebert said he would attempt to send Lonnie Weeks to the electric chair. Louis Dukes would be tried as an accomplice. He couldn't be sentenced to death, but could receive life in prison.

In 1993, some capital murder crime victims had begun to give impact statements at the sentencing phase of trials, and Mr. Ebert wanted to rehearse questions that he might ask if I testified in court.

In 1991, the Supreme Court of the United States considered the victim impact statement as a form of testimony that was allowable during the sentencing phase of a trial (in Payne v. Tennessee 501 U.S. 808 (1991).

The court ruled that the admission of such statements did not violate the U.S. Constitution and that the statements could be ruled as admissible in death penalty cases.

I decided I could give a statement because I wanted to share the murder's effects on me.

I also made the decision to attend the trial each day, to be a voice for José.

I was nervous as the trial approached. But I knew I had to get through the process. I could not "cop out" emotionally or appear to be a desperate spouse.

The trial began on October 19, 1993, almost eight months after José was killed. As television cameras arrived inside the courtroom, a cameraman spared me publicity by seating me away from the camera.

Captain Howard Gregory of the Virginia State Police attended every day. Other state police officers from José's barracks attended the trial on various days.

My brother-in-law, Donald Falls, sat with me daily and was my faithful supporter and friend.

When I faced Lonnie Weeks in court that opening day of the trial, I had no feeling for him. He said that the Devil made him shoot, a strong force took over his body and mind. He was under a spell.

My mind was still stone cold. I was still numb. I had neither good nor bad feelings for the defendant. Lonnie Weeks was in my periphery for as long as he lived, and that is where he is today.

In the very beginning when I realized José was murdered and in all the years that followed, I never hated

Lonnie Weeks, but I wanted him to pay for murdering my husband. I grieved for José with the deepest despair, and I realized I had no energy left to hate. Perhaps this preserved my sanity. I don't know.

I wondered who else to blame. I couldn't blame José for having a dangerous job and not realizing the danger that February morning. I blamed the murderers and believed that Weeks and Dukes should be punished.

I knew Weeks and Dukes were young men who had made a bad choice. The prosecutor reminded the jury that premeditation requires only seconds. Ebert strongly suggested that Weeks and Dukes premeditated the murder before Dukes exited the car and walked to the rear of the vehicle to be frisked.

Random details of the trial filter through my mind much like an early news reel. It has been many years since the trial, but newspaper articles I have kept and my frequent journaling refresh the details for me.

I remember Assistant Prosecutor James Willett pointing the Glock weapon in court when he demonstrated the stance Weeks probably used to fire the gun. I gasped when I saw José's bloody body armor, the Kevlar vest that didn't save his life. I cringed as Trooper Douglas Buchanan, who administered CPR, explained in his testimony that air came out of holes in my husband's chest when he blew his breath into his mouth.

I fled the courtroom, unable to listen further when the medical examiner Dr. Carol McMahon testified, "One of the fatal rounds hit Cavazos above the right collarbone, severed two major arteries that carry blood from the heart, and pieced a lung before exiting through the left side of his body."

During Weeks' testimony, he said he thought to throw the gun out of the car when my husband asked Dukes to exit the car, but decided to use it.

The court-appointed defense lawyer had no case, because his client had confessed.

The courtroom drama lasted a week, short for a capital murder trial, but it exhausted me.

The jury deliberated thirty minutes.

I saw their looks of stress. They really didn't want their job. Many hung their heads as the guilty verdict was read. Some cried.

In January of the next year, the sentencing phase began.

I sobbed as I gave my victim statement. I had hoped I wouldn't cry, but I did.

I explained the shock I felt to be living when José was dead. I couldn't eat or get up in the morning. My emotions would quickly swing from sorrow to joy.

Often years later when I laughed, I would cry at the same time. It is a unnerving experience to feel sorrow at the same moment of feeling joy.

José's fellow troopers filled two rows in the courtroom and waited to hear the sentence.

Weeks was sentenced to death.

There were sighs of relief, but no joy. Everyone in the courtroom recalled José's life and untimely death. The troopers revered him and said his best attribute was friendliness.

Perhaps his friendly nature contributed to his death.

Louis Jefferson Dukes, Jr. was offered a plea bargain that encouraged him to take a second-degree murder charge. He wanted to have a trial.

On November 16, 1993, shortly after the Weeks trial, the two-day, non-jury trial for Louis Dukes began.

The judge found him guilty of first-degree murder, a verdict that carried life with eligibility of parole.

He is still in prison.

I call every year to learn if he has been released.

10

Execution

Execution n. a) carrying out, doing,
producing b) a putting to death as in
accordance with a legally imposed sentence

The two definitions of the word "execution" are polar opposites. On the one hand, the word suggests moving forward, completing tasks, being productive. It can also mean putting an end to life.

After the crime, I believe my life took on the characteristics of the first definition. I was determined to move on.

The completion of the two trials was not a blissful turning point or an open road to family joy and happiness. The children and I lived on, each of us affected differently by the murder.

I know the children were overwhelmed as I was by their father's murder. That fall, my son entered his senior year of high school and my daughter began her senior year of college. In spite of their grief they lived on, went to school, enjoyed friends, and did well.

The holidays were sad, primarily because José was born on Christmas Day.

My sister invited us for the first few Christmas holidays to her home in Richmond, and that helped us avoid trying to celebrate in a home that was so altered, where life was so empty without José.

I returned to work ten days after the funeral. Work provided productivity, I had wonderful co-workers, and my boss Nyla Papiernik was a huge support. On days that I burst out in tears at my desk, head in my hands, Nyla gave me comfort. I will always be thankful for her loving friendship.

I took a big leap, was really brave, when at the age of fifty-one, I returned to college to earn my degree.

Virginia had passed a law that allowed free tuition at state-supported colleges to survivors of line-of-duty deaths.

At my daughter's encouragement, I applied to George Mason University in Fairfax, Virginia. They accepted me in their Government and Politics degree program. And I received credits from the two years I attended the College of William & Mary thirty years before.

My first evening course was Economics. I was scared and had to force myself to walk into the classroom. I didn't want to fail in this endeavor. I wanted to continue changing my life, remaining strong and focused.

Luckily, I was in class with a mixture of young students and many older students who returned to college for a second degree, so I didn't elicit too many stares.

I graduated *cum laude* two years later in December 1997, fulfilling a goal set in my early twenties.

Returning to college provided purpose to my life, challenged me, and brought new friends.

Time went by, tearful memorials came and went, and healing came step by step for us.

Despite the fact that Virginia executes death row inmates quickly, Lonnie Weeks was still alive seven years after his conviction.

His defense team questioned the penalty verdict and appealed it to the United States Supreme Court.

At question was the two-day penalty phase of the capital murder in which Weeks was found guilty.

The prosecution wanted to prove two aggravating circumstances that called for the death penalty: 1. That the defendant would be likely to commit criminal acts that would be a threat to society, and 2. That the defendant's conduct was "outrageously or wantonly vile, horrible or inhuman, in that it involved depravity of mind or aggravated battery."

The case before the U.S. Supreme Court (No. 99-5746) presented the question of whether the U.S. Constitution was violated if a judge directed a capital jury's attention to a specific paragraph of a constitutionally sufficient instruction in response to a question regarding proper judgment of mitigating circumstances.

The jury in the case on the second day of deliberations asked, "Does the sentence of life imprisonment in the State of Virginia have the possibility of parole, and if so, what conditions must be met to receive parole?"

The judge explained to the jury, "You should impose such punishment as you feel is just under the evidence, and within the instructions of the Court. You are not to concern yourselves with what may happen afterwards."

That afternoon, the jury posed another question. "If we believe that Lonnie Weeks, Jr. is guilty of at least 1 of the alternatives, then is it our duty as a jury to issue the death penalty? Or must we decide (even though he is guilty of one of the alternatives) whether or not to issue the death penalty, or one of the life sentences? What is the Rule? Please clarify?"

The judge's answer to the jury's question referred to the jury's written instructions. "In instruction number 2 that was given to them, in the second paragraph, it reads, 'If you find from the evidence that the Commonwealth has proved, beyond a reasonable doubt, either of the two alternatives, and as to that alternative, you are unanimous, then you may fix the punishment of the defendant at death, or if you believe from all the evidence that the death penalty is not justified, then you shall fix the punishment of the defendant at imprisonment for life, or imprisonment for life with a fine not to exceed $100,000.'"

Two hours after the judge's instruction to the jury, this decision was read: "We the jury, on the issue joined, having found the defendant Lonnie Weeks, Jr., guilty of capital murder, and having unanimously found that his conduct in committing the offense is outrageously or wantonly vile, horrible or inhumane, in that it involved depravity of mind and/or aggravated battery, and having considered the evidence in mitigation of the offense, unanimously fix his punishment at death."

Supreme Court Chief Justice Rehnquist delivered the opinion of the court on January 20, 2000.

Five justices affirmed the court's penalty verdict, and four dissented.

The result was that by one vote, the U.S. Supreme Court upheld Weeks' death sentence.

Part of the court's opinion read, "Given that petitioner's jury was adequately instructed, and given that the trial judge responded to the jury's question by directing its attention to the precise paragraph of the constitutionally adequate instruction that answers its inquiry, the question becomes whether the Constitution requires anything more. We hold that it does not."

Justice Stevens wrote the dissenting opinion. He felt

with "virtual certainty" that the jury did not realize that "even if they found one of those circumstances, they did not have a 'duty as a jury' to issue the death penalty."

The execution was scheduled for March 16, 2000.

I wasn't aware that my children started a campaign to commute the sentence and block the execution. My daughter wrote to then Governor James Gilmore asking him to spare Weeks' life:

"Will his death bring my father back from the dead? Will it set the record straight? Will I, his child, feel less grief? The answer is 'no.'

"Please take into consideration the feelings my brother and I have in this matter. We have thought about this very carefully. In our hearts, we have forgiven all that has been done to our family."

Some press communication supported the Cavazos children's appeal to spare Weeks' own two children the pain of losing a father. The Cavazos siblings didn't want to be vengeful.

Again, we were in the public spotlight. But this time, the family was split. The children asked to stop the execution and I wanted to proceed. The press was in a frenzy.

An execution was overwhelming for the children. They wanted closure on their terms.

I eventually made a statement that my children were entitled to their opinion. Who would ever expect to have to face the execution of the killer of your husband, or your father?

I felt compelled to support the death sentence in support of state police and all law enforcement people who are in danger every day. I knew other officers would die violently by gunfire and there would be other trials.

But it was too late to turn the tide. As scheduled, on March 16 Weeks died by lethal injection at the Greensville Corrections Center in Jarratt, Virginia.

Governor Gilmore's response to the public was, "Trooper José Cavazos died honorably in the performance of his duties while protecting the lives of the people of Virginia. Weeks admitted to police that he murdered Trooper Cavazos. I decline to intervene."

Weeks' grandmother stated that her grandson knew that the Cavazos children forgave him, and he was at peace before he died.

No one in our family witnessed the execution. We were represented by personnel from the state police.

11

Second Marriage

As I described earlier in this narrative, in the biblical story about Adam and Eve, God created man and woman to live together, as "soul mates," and I started to want that again in my life; I wanted marriage.

I talked to myself because José's influence was still present. But I knew he couldn't answer me, and that made me angry. I had to remind myself that he surely couldn't help me make a decision.

What was it that I missed when I was single for all those years? It took me two years to even consider "dating."

As I said before, I was timid and it was hard for me to sell myself, to have confidence. I lost a big part of my ego that day José died. I was pretty certain I had good attributes to share, but I found it difficult to show my true feelings.

Finally, I started to notice men that attracted me. How could I forget José's kiss and hugs, his teasing, and of course I missed making love with a man. I was tired of sleeping alone. It wasn't the life I was used to.

Once my son went to college in 1995, there was no one at the dinner table anymore, and no conversation at home after work or when I came home from college classes. If I wanted conversation, I called my children or my friends, or I met close female friends for dinner.

Several widowers in the area whom José and I both knew approached me after their wives died.

One was a great guy, and we took swing dance lessons and had some fun. I remember going out for New Year's Eve with him. It was a huge deal for me to have a date for New Year's Eve. I had been alone so very long. But he and his wife had been my friends, and I couldn't accept dating someone simply because it was convenient. Besides, he never asked me to marry him.

Always a romantic, I was determined to be in crazy love again. I wouldn't settle for less.

Sometimes I would go to mixers with single groups. It wasn't fun. Talking to a lot of folks with whom you had nothing in common was disappointing. It wore me out.

I was also approached by some married men. That was quite a shock, since I was always faithful to my husband. I heard men's stories of being unhappy at home.

I definitely didn't want a married man in my life, at least one not married to me. I didn't need any more pain and sorrow and empty hopes.

After six years as a widow, I joined a dating match service. I signed on through the telephone at home. The dating service was sponsored by a radio station, long before the Internet was "everywhere" and before Match.com.

I used the keypad to enter a profile, including age, education, how many children I had, on and on. I was able to leave a brief voice message for anyone who listened.

I weeded men out, but eventually Ron and I started dating.

Ron was divorced and had two children. His daughter was twenty-two and his son was twenty. Ron was friendly, my friends and family liked him, and he was nice-looking.

I fell in love with him. I believed I had waited ample

time and had made a good decision to remarry. I wish his ex-wife had given me a call, but I was too much in love to change my mind.

We got married in May 2000. Our wedding was held in St. James Episcopal Church in Leesburg, Virginia. Our adult children were attendants.

The ceremony was classy. We had communion and the organist played the Wedding March and several hymns. A friend whom I had never heard sing offered to sing during the ceremony. Her voice was beautiful and classical.

I bought the flowers for the wedding party and church altar at a local flower farm in Leesburg. There were peonies and stargazer lilies in our bouquets. The flowers were tied with a satin bow. I still remember their fragrance.

I wore a two-piece formal gown. The top was ivory lace and the skirt was a full, tan taffeta. I adored the dress and had invested much time selecting it. My friend Becky Wilson helped me shop. That dress is still hanging, in a bag, in my extra closet. I cannot let it go.

We hosted our own formal dinner. We had a tasty butter cream/strawberry cake, an open bar, and a DJ.

We honeymooned in Maine and spent several nights in Boston. I was so enthralled with life again and had happy expectations for us. I was excited to plan to retire with Ron.

He worked in Washington, DC and I was working in Leesburg. We lived in the home I had built while I was single.

I won't share the money details that we each brought to the marriage. But Ron seemed content that I paid my own bills, and I did help him pay off debt he acquired from his divorce.

Two years into our marriage, he retired from his union job and we bought a bed-and-breakfast in a small city called Williams, Arizona near the Grand Canyon.

The business was difficult to manage, and it was impossible to make any profit in the early days. But we soon started to roll in revenue and guests.

We cooked breakfasts, cleaned the kitchen each morning, and got the rooms turned over for the newcomers checking in that afternoon.

The work was stressful because the home was 5000 square feet, and when the cleaning person didn't come to work, we would do all the labor.

The cleaning help required constant managing. Our standard for room cleaning was very high. We insisted rooms be sanitized and CLEAN.

I did the accounting, took reservations, ran deposits, and managed our website. Business decisions were discussed by both of us and we tried to agree on expenditures.

Ron did the maintenance on the home, which was endless. He also worked part time some of those years in Arizona.

Ron drank too much.

I knew he drank beer when we were dating. One night during our first weeks of dating, he brought a twelve-pack to my home. I started to wonder about this habit, but I wanted to marry, so I suppose I turned a "blind eye" to who he was. He never appeared a nasty or sloppy drunk, and that's what tricked me.

He consumed four or five beers every evening, and sometimes more. I actually believed beer was safe, that no one became an alcoholic from beer.

Late in the summer of 2010, I took a trip to help my daughter.

Ron was being left with the business to manage and working part time when he could. As he helped me load the car, I saw a strange look in his eyes that I will never forget.

When I came home from that trip, I didn't recognize his usual facial expressions. He was totally different and very confrontational.

We had had arguments, usually about money, drinking, and women.

He always skirted any problems that I brought up about revenue or how to stretch business gains to do renovations or minor repairs. He would tell me I was too controlling.

And after eventually getting tired of the constant beer bottles and the nightly habit, I would ask him to cut back on the drinking. Once I asked him to stop drinking on Sundays to give me a rest from the constant distress.

I suggested he go away for the next weekend to make him feel less stressed. At that getaway weekend, I found he had met a woman in Phoenix. He told me he was going to gamble in Laughlin, Nevada, but my private investigator who I hired from an internet search, tracked him to a golf resort in Phoenix.

The next day, the investigator handed me pictures of them coming out of a restaurant in Phoenix. They departed in two cars, but first gave each other a big kiss.

What a blow.

For about a year, I never knew who the woman was, but later Ron admitted it was a lady who he had done a handyman job for in Doney Park, near Flagstaff. Her name was Evelyn, and her husband had been injured in an electrical accident and was handicapped.

Ron would talk to me about her paying him with fists of cash. I could tell he was excited about all her cash.

I had been seeing a counselor earlier that summer to discuss issues about money and how I usually carried a bigger financial responsibility for our personal expenses. I was getting pretty burnt out.

After I knew Ron's drinking problems were impossible to deal with and that he had this "fling" going on, I spoke one more time to the marriage/addiction counselor.

I moved beyond the money issues and discussed showing her the photos of Ron and his girlfriend. And I described his drinking issues through our ten-year marriage.

She immediately told me in a firm voice, "Your husband is an alcoholic and has other addictions."

She explained that most alcoholics have more than one addiction. Ron's second addiction was he sought out other women.

My counselor said that I could stay with him and try to make him "well," or I could leave him and make a life alone if I thought I could be happy.

I knew that was the line she often told people. But her advice was like picking up a hot poker.

The first few nights after my return from helping my daughter, Ron stayed in one of the guest rooms. And each morning, I found about nine beer bottles in the closet.

He was beyond listening to advice or being able to solve our problems. He was on a downward roll.

One night, he screamed about all the faults he thought I had. The next day, I called my sister and told her I was sure I was going to die.

Soon after I returned from that trip, he asked for a divorce.

To make this story brief and spare all the sad details, I will just reveal that I was sobbing when he asked for a divorce.

Despite all the warning signs, it was a huge shock.

Within a month, Ron rescinded his divorce decree against me.

But as our relationship deteriorated and after two orders of protection against him and other horrible incidents I endured, I really didn't have the energy to make him well.

I filed for divorce in April 2011.

During the divorce proceedings, I had no family in Arizona and needed advice. So I consulted a grief counselor.

My counselor explained that both with the death of my first husband and now in this divorce process, I had experienced two dark nights of the soul.

A dark night of the soul is when our life crashes and burns. Nothing is left, except the ashes of a past life and for some, a broken heart.

The counselor affirmed that renewal eventually happens, and joy replaces the sadness and grief. A dark night is part of the natural process of living, he said, and no one should feel stigmatized.

But it took a long time before I accepted that the processes that caused the loss of one husband by death and another because of alcoholism were natural human experiences.

I questioned why twice in my life I had lost all stability.

Since I had already lost one husband who had been murdered, I was afraid to divorce and do what I knew I should do. I feared being alone again.

Fear pulled me back and shadowed my decisions. I was scared.

I tried hard to "fix" my feelings.

I listened to a CD my counselor encouraged me to buy: "The Four Agreements" by Don Miguel Ruiz. It offered an explanation of how to live the Toltec life.

Toltecs believed that our brains dream all the time. However, each human is part of God and shines an individual light into the world. Each must master his own life and dreams and become independent, free from what society dictates as correct living.

If people can control their own freedom, then they can have heaven on earth. One does not have to die to experience heaven.

The author encouraged readers to shed the role of victim and the fear that holds us back from being productive individuals when bad things happen. Most importantly, grieving individuals must not become victims.

Crucially, I decided I had been preyed upon.

Life became different for me. I opened my heart to new possibilities and tried to live with an open, loving heart.

I tried to be someone with an upbeat outlook, whom others would like. I tried to smile even when bad memories overtook my thoughts.

After the turmoil and pain I endured, I wanted to live with love and compassion for others. I particularly wanted my children and later their children to feel my inner glow, even though so many times I faked it.

I looked forward to unknowable twists my life might take. I had freed myself from the expectations of others and depended on my own judgment.

I still had my low moments, hours of loneliness and unyielding pain, but little by little, I began to rise above the ashes of my past.

12

My Spirit and My Love

…we have to recognize that we are spiritual beings with souls existing in a spiritual world as well as material beings with bodies and brains in a material world.
— Sir John C. Eccles, *Evolution of the Brain: Creation of the Self*, 1989. p. 241

Please do not minimize the importance of my story, which I dedicate to other victims of violence or others who have lost someone they loved.

I faced many years of unending hurdles, but I am determined to share my feelings and be proud of my life.

Before José died, my nature was somewhat passive. I was timid but when pushed too far, I always fought for myself.

I had to fight for my integrity with him on occasion or I would have been pushed aside. It was stressful, and José was very aggressive since he was a strong male chauvinist.

I challenged myself during the early years of raising my children. I was the loving mother, and I would try to protect my children from the tough love he administered. He would lecture the children explaining why choosing correct decisions was not easy, raise his voice when he believed they made mistakes. He loved us, but all too often, it his way or the highway.

He wanted five children, and I wanted two. We had two.

When I was left to live alone, I gravitated to the repressed inner strength I had silently cultivated all my married life.

My house was on six acres and a lot to manage. I mowed my acre of grass with the riding mower. I kept the house functioning, stoked the wood stove in the basement, and ordered and stacked firewood.

I nurtured our two cats and German shepherd, Anastasia, who missed José. He always took the back path to the house when he returned from work. She listened for his footsteps coming down that pathway long after he died.

After José died, I worked full time because I had to. The children were a huge priority for me. I tried to be both parents, which wasn't possible.

I had to force myself to adopt a good use of money and save what I could to assure stability for all three of us, and more recently just for myself.

Putting investments in the stock market was risky, and markets were swinging wildly some years. I lost investments in market downturns.

I probably spent too much money. Now that I am retired, I wish I had done a better job saving. But I always tried to respect what I received as a result of José's death.

In 1997, I sold the house we raised the children in. The house and lot were becoming a burden. Trees would fall into the yard around the perimeter of the grass and would have to be removed. It was isolated, recessed from the main road. I knew few of the neighbors because my children's friends were growing up and leaving home. But most of all, it held too many memories for me and I was lonely.

I oversaw the construction of a house in another county.

Then in 2002, I sold that house and bought the bed-and-breakfast in Arizona.

I became an entrepreneur for the first time in my life. My second husband and I did well with that business, and we learned so much.

The material world was ever-present, but I was losing touch with what the Nobel Prize-winning neurophysiologist John C. Eccles called the spiritual world.

In my English class at George Mason University, Viktor Frankl's *Man's Search for Meaning* was required reading. Frankl, a survivor of the Nazi concentration camps, suggested steps by which a person could recover from profound loss.

Loss could be death of a loved one, loss of home, loss of personal possessions, or loss of country. But importantly, he wrote, "Love is the ultimate and highest goal to which man can aspire. Love goes very far beyond the physical person of the beloved…whether or not he is alive at all."

Jews lost family members to the death camps during WWII, and through his book Frankl taught how to overcome profound sadness. It is a useful book for anyone suffering tragedy.

Dr. Eben Alexander, M.D., in his book *Proof of Heaven*, wrote that each human needs to be in touch with the spiritual aspect of self. He wrote how he was in a coma and almost died. His brain showed no activity for a long time. His story is of being in heaven, and what he experienced. "Love is, without a doubt, the basis of everything… the day-to-day kind that everyone knows–the kind of love we feel when we look at our spouse or our children. It is the purest and most powerful form."

Dr. Alexander stressed that we need to bring our spirit to life. Each person can "get in closer to this genuine spiritual self by manifesting love and compassion. These two traits make up the fabric of a spiritual realm."

Both Frankl and Alexander wrote of the importance of a spiritual reckoning. Both felt that without a loving heart, a person's inner growth is restricted. The answer is love.

As Jesus tried to teach us, "Love one another."

I was healed by my own determination and by gleaning strength from within, but I definitely counted on my family and friends for compassion and support.

I prayed every morning and felt a strong presence enfolding me. I couldn't have lived had God not been with me, but it was through dreams and other unexplainable events that I found peace.

The first extraordinary dream I had was in the 1970s. I was young with two small children and José was still alive.

In my dream, I opened a door and a person in a hooded cloak faced me. The face was in shadows, not recognizable. This small, strange figure handed me a white rose.

I awoke frightened.

Later that morning, José received a phone call from his family in Texas. He was told his mother had died during the night.

In 1993 in the first months after José died, I dreamt very little about him. My sleep was so fitful and when I woke, it was with a startled jerk. I would lie awake for hours and had no sleep patterns for months.

But later that summer, I had dreams that included

intense feelings.

It was early June and I was home from work, sick, and asleep on my sofa.

Then I felt a force around my head and torso, a surrounding of my body. I had no sense of fear. I was calm.

I believe José visited me that time. Was he worried that I was ill?

That October, I dreamt again. Soon after falling asleep, I felt that José was in bed beside me, just like when he lived with me. He was hugging me, his arms around my torso, and he gave me one of his warm kisses.

I believe he was there as he had been for the twenty-three years of our life together. Did he come back for me, just briefly?

January the next year, I dreamt I saw José in his uniform, his body looking stiff because he had on his bulletproof vest–that didn't save his life.

I felt a force field and a pull on my body. His energy force was surrounding me.

José had been deceased for more than two years. I hadn't "felt" his aura for some time, but in October 1996, I dreamt we were young and in our first home, a small ranch house in Richmond.

I saw him in the bedroom, and I told him he was dead.

He said, "No, I am back for a while."

I was in bed, but we didn't touch.

I remember my confusion because he had been gone so long and I had the feeling of being abandoned.

Near the end of my dream, he changed form and seemed to convert to a small wooden symbol. The symbol flew by my head into the space above and disappeared.

Fourteen years later in September 2010, it was the beginning of the end of my second marriage. I realized Ron was an addict and in the process of abandoning our marriage.

I was distraught and didn't go home that night. I was sobbing and alone in a motel.

I slept fitfully, but awoke in the night. In light that filtered up from the streetlights below, I saw an entity. It had a bodily form, but wasn't distinguishable as a person.

I wasn't afraid, but very calm.

It transferred words to me, "Do not be afraid. I am here."

I blinked and sat up, but soon fell back to sleep.

The next day, I remembered what I had experienced.

I knew that this connection from another realm meant I was receiving spiritual help. Someone heard my plight, my anguish, and reached out to me.

Who was it? I wish I knew.

But now I know in our deepest despair, a light can shine.

13

Awareness of Gun Violence

Let's FINISH THE JOB we started 20 years ago and expand background checks to all gun sales, including gun show and online sales.

–Dan Gross
The Brady Campaign to
Prevent Gun Violence
June 10, 2014

On March 23, 1993, my children and I were invited to a bill-signing by Virginia Governor Douglas Wilder. He was the commonwealth's first black governor and a gracious person.

I dressed in a new mid-calf navy dress with a white collar, accented by blue heels, but the battle inside me showed in my face.

My daughter made the trip to Richmond from her college. My son was in a sport coat. shirt, and tie. His blond hair was long and in a ponytail. His dad wouldn't have been happy about his son's hair.

The law was named the Cavazos-Draughn Law. Mr. Draughn was a security officer shot to death in a McDonald's parking lot in Richmond in January 1993.

At that time, Virginia was called the gunrunning capital of the U.S. The bill allowed residents to purchase just one handgun a month when previously there had been no restrictions on gun purchases.

Other bills signed that day 1) prohibited juveniles from possessing handguns except for target shooting, 2) delayed driving privileges for two years to juveniles convicted of possession of a concealed weapon, and 3) set a two-year sentence for people convicted of buying guns for resale, called straw purchases.

The gun used to kill José had been used in a murder in North Carolina in January 1993, but there was no trace of any registration for the gun. The police investigated and tried to find any information on the gun's history before Weeks obtained it. Nothing was found.

José was licensed to carry a firearm after becoming a Virginia State Trooper. But he had never drawn his weapon against anyone. I think if he were alive today, he would support passing stringent gun laws.

It's as though policemen are shot by people carrying multiple weapons or shot by people who should be blocked from having a gun at all.

If in 1993 our gun laws were tougher, José might still be alive.

It is ironic that in the 1990s, Virginia was passing laws to prohibit gun ownership by juveniles and children. Currently students are being killed by other young people who usually own numerous guns and abundant ammunition.

Since José's death, the United States has experienced increasing gun violence, which affects families every day.

Yet laws haven't leveled the playing field for the victims, and victims don't have options to fight back.

While this is a problem that calls for change, legislators balk at restricting gun purchases and supporting more stringent background checks.

The violent trend toward mass murders began on April 20, 1999, when teenagers Eric Harris and Dylan Kiebold "shot up" Columbine High School, killing 13 and wounding 21 others.

Who can forget the news coverage that documented children fleeing the scene, crying, embracing parents who waited for them with frozen hope? How lucky were those parents who escaped the heartache of death, grief, and tragedy? But some parents experienced the tragic loss of a murdered child.

Dave Cullen's book *Columbine* includes what Tom Mauser said after the death of his son, Daniel, at a National Rifle Association show attended by 4,000: "Something is wrong when a child can grab a gun so easily."

The intent of the young killers at Columbine was to use pipe bombs for a massive loss of life. But the largest bomb they brought onto school property never detonated. So they turned to their backup plan: guns.

After Columbine, similar scenes of carnage followed all too often.

On July 29, 1999, Mark Barton murdered his family and then shot and killed 9 others at a trading company.

On July 8, 2000, Doug Williams shot persons in a Lockheed plant, where 7 died.

On July 20, 2012, during a premiere of the movie *Dark Knight Rises*, James Holmes killed 12 people and wounded 58.

On April 16, 2007, Virginia Tech had the deadliest school shooting rampage ever, when Seung-Hui Choi gunned down 56, and 32 of those people died.

One of the most horrific events happened on

December 14, 2012, when Adam Lanza shot 20 very young children and 5 staff members at Sandy Hook Elementary School. Before he terrorized the school, he killed his mother.

Even members of Congress have felt the savage use of firearms, when on January 8, 2011, Jared Loughner, started shooting at a political gathering, at a Safeway store parking area in Tucson, Arizona. 6 people died as a result, and the Arizona State Representative, Gabby Giffords, was badly injured.

The Brady Handgun Violence Prevention Act (The Brady Law) was signed by President Clinton on November 30, 1993.

Sarah Brady worked hard for the law's enactment after her husband James Brady was shot during the attempted assassination of President Ronald Regan on March 30, 1981.

Jim Brady spoke at the signing ceremony, "Twelve years ago, my life was changed forever by a disturbed young man with a gun. Until that time, I hadn't thought much about gun control. Maybe if I had, I would not be stuck with these wheels."

Jim Brady did live, but sustained numerous injuries. He died in August 2014. Nick Corasaniti wrote, in the *New York Times* on August 8, 2014, "The coroner ruled Brady's death a homicide." That is, his death was a result of being shot in 1981.

The Brady Law required conducting background checks on individuals before a firearm was purchased from a federally licensed dealer, manufacturer, or importer, unless an exception applied. In his book *Columbine*, author Dave Cullen stressed that the loophole in the Brady Law was that mandatory checks did not apply at gun shows.

According to the law, a firearm could be purchased if a person had an acceptable record in the National Instant Criminal Background Check System.

There are nine standards by which one can be denied a gun purchase. They include being convicted in court and imprisoned for more than a year, being a fugitive from justice, addiction to a controlled substance, dishonorable discharge from the military, and being adjudicated as a mental defective or committed to a mental facility.

Clearly, given the number of weapons mass murderers have used in the killings, people who shouldn't possess guns are readily able to buy them.

On the flip side, the National Rifle Association and gun ownership advocates believe that disarming good citizens is not the answer.

On February 4, 1989, Don Kates, Jr. wrote in the *New York Times*, "Violence will be decreased only by painful, basic, long-term change in the socio-economic and cultural factors that produce such a high number of violence-prone individuals in society."

On September 28, 1995, the Centers for Disease Control and Prevention (CDC) defined a new disease and gave it a name that embraced its impetus: "violence." The CDC defined violence as "spousal abuse, wrongful homicide, assault, other violent crimes, and suicide." The CDC acknowledged that gun ownership was a risky business to be reckoned with.

Dr. Lindsay Gibson, a clinical psychologist, wrote a feature article titled "Passing for Normal" in the July 2014 edition of *Tidewater Women*. She described how those who committed the country's most recent mass murders for the most part appeared normal to those interfacing with them.

She attributed mass murder to an attachment disorder. Many of these killers are easy to overlook by professionals, yet their thoughts become more violent daily. Both killers at the Columbine incident had been in counseling several times.

Many murderers commit mass killings to feel interaction with large groups, because their personal interaction with peers has been limited all their lives.

Dr. Gibson warned that educators, parents, and law enforcement have to learn to identify potential mass killers before it is too late, before they act out their anger.

The right to bear arms, which is protected by the Second Amendment of the U.S. Constitution, may have outlived its purpose. Ratified on December 17, 1791 along with nine other amendments that make up the Bill of Rights, this short amendment is open to interpretation. Specifically, its exact meaning in terms of what types of weapons are protected is still in contention today.

The Second Amendment reads: "A well regulated Militia, being necessary to the security of a free State, the right of the people to keep and bear Arms, shall not be infringed." This sentence can be interpreted in numerous ways and raises many questions.

The Second Amendment was passed in the United States' early history, before "the West was won," before the frontier was tamed. In the 21st Century, should guns be available only to the military and law enforcement?

For those gun owners who pass the requirements of owning a gun, should they also have the right to buy as many guns as they want? Should we reinstate the ban on assault weapons?

Can we better understand the socio-economic factors that make people act out with violence? How much violence can we prevent?

Let's be aware of the impersonal lives so many of the children in this country live, perhaps because of social media. Why are more and more children becoming aggressive, growing up without a conscience, and killing others?

The answers are hard to find, but we cannot let violence and mass killings continue. Any victim who has lost a loved one would probably agree.

After the Sandy Hook Elementary School shootings, President Obama said, "We won't be able to stop every violent act, but if there is even one thing that we can do to prevent any of these events, we have an obligation to try."

He continued, "We cannot and will not be passive in the face of such violence. We should be willing to challenge old assumptions in order to lessen the prospects of such violence again."

The federal Assault Weapons Ban was in force for ten years, between 1994 and 2004. After 2004, the law was no longer in force, and I thought immediately that allowing the ban to expire was a huge mistake.

In 2016, three police officers in Baton Rouge, Louisiana and five officers in Dallas, Texas were shot to death. In both instances, crazed men brandished AR-15 assault rifles.

José's violent death forced me to think about gun violence decades ago. I lobbied for gun regulations in the 1990s in the Virginia General Assembly. It was as though the issue was in my face, and I hoped to help solve the problem.

This century's survivors of gun violence continue to work for legislation to limit firearm ownership.

14

Fighting for
Survivors' Benefits

The week after José's funeral, Danny Blankenship, the Human Resource Director of the Virginia State Police, arrived at my home with several officers of the state police. My brother-in-law Don Falls was by my side.

I began to understand the amount of money I would receive from José's life insurance policy and disbursements from the Virginia Line of Duty Act and the Federal Public Safety Officers' Benefit. I wouldn't be wealthy, but I would be stable if I was smart.

My mind was churning and I was afraid because I was now sole parent of two older children, one already in college and one approaching college.

To our benefit, Virginia law allowed children and spouses of police officers killed on duty to have free tuition for college at any state-supported university course if they were accepted by the college. The law provided valuable assistance because my daughter was attending a state-supported university. My son and I would later take advantage of that law.

Also, I would receive part of José's pension, although the pension amount would have an offset with workers' compensation payments. Workers' compensation lasted for ten years, but stopped if a surviving spouse remarried, a red flag in those days.

Worse, I learned from the Human Resources director that health insurance premiums for my family would cost almost half of José's pension amount.

I was becoming concerned and boldly left the others at my dining room table to call the chaplain of the state police, who always gave me good advice.

I was frightened and decided to try to manage my future. I took off my timid hat and started the hard work to change laws, with the help of people in charge. After all, I had lost years of earning power from a husband who was now dead.

After that day, I talked to lobbyist Bill Ellwood from the Virginia State Police several times. I became acquainted with Charles J. Colgan, a state senator from Prince William County who promised to support changing line of duty benefits.

In March 1994 a year after José died, Virginia Senate Bill 609 was approved, granting that my family's health insurance would be provided by the state.

Virginia State Senator Edgar S. Robb from Charlottesville sponsored the bill in the upper house of the General Assembly, and Virginia State Delegate H. Russell Potts, Jr. sponsored it in the House of Delegates.

Part of the text follows:

"Whereas, Virginia State Trooper José M Cavazos was killed in the line of duty on February 24, 1993 while in service to the Commonwealth; and

"Whereas, Trooper Cavazos left behind a wife, Linda M. Cavazos of Nokesville, Virginia, and two children who were dependent on his ability to provide income and other benefits, including health insurance...

"Whereas, the Commonwealth and its citizens owe the surviving family of Trooper Cavazos a great debt of gratitude and compassion to the ultimate sacrifice he made on behalf of Virginia...

"1. That provisions shall be made to continue the family health insurance coverage as provided under 2.1-20.1 of the Code of Virginia for the surviving widow, Linda M. Cavazos of Nokesville, Virginia, and children of Trooper Cavazos until such time as any of the following shall occur..."

Two of the provisions were that I would lose coverage if I remarried or bought different health insurance.

In May 2000 after remarrying, I lost my health insurance coverage.

But it was reinstated by a new law on July 1, 2000. The new Code of Virginia Section 2.1-133.7:1 granted every family member who lost a spouse or father or mother in the line of duty continued health insurance coverage and removed the remarriage restriction.

The Virginia State Police lobbyist Bill Ellwood and State Senator Charles Colgan worked hard to encourage passage of the bill.

When I remarried in May 2000, I also lost José's pension.

I never understood why benefits should be taken away from a police survivor when he or she decided to remarry. It's an old adage that a new spouse can "take care of" a survivor. Most often, there are still children to raise and leftover financial damages from losing a partner in a horrific manner.

Mr. Ellwood and State Senator Colgan worked for change for many years.

I and other Concerns of Police Survivors (COPS) members just kept making calls and writing letters.

I was shocked when I got the news on July 1, 2000

that Governor Gilmore struck the remarriage clause from the line of duty survivor pension bill. With the signing of Senate Bill 415, all other widows or widowers were saved the frustration of losing pension benefits if he or she remarried.

I was thrilled not only for myself, but also for everyone.

Survivors who lost a police officer in the line of duty after 1993 might not realize what work it took to change this restrictive clause for all Virginia line of duty survivors.

I know that the several senators I mentioned made this happen, along with lobbyists for the state police.

The change in laws helped me survive financially. I was able to finish raising my children free from money worries. I was able to finish my college education. And most importantly, I remained independent to manage my own affairs.

15

Breath of Life

It felt hardest in the morning as I faced a new day, and remembered how difficult it was to live the hours of a changed life. When I awoke, most often at dawn, I sometimes remembered the dreams of that night. Often my dreams held his face, and I experienced the joy of his memory and felt a moment of peace. As I embraced that memory and arose, I moved with guarded hope, and asked God to be with me.

–From my notes in a writing class at Grace and Holy Trinity Cathedral in Kansas City, Missouri (2014)

I often think about that person I would have become if José had not been killed.

José could never understand the energy it took for me to say good-bye, to let him go. But I'm sure he would be pleased that I survived without him these many years.

It's still a work in progress, this life of mine. I consider choices before making significant changes. I have learned to respect myself and make changes alone.

I felt compelled to share my story. It was cathartic for me to revisit the details of the aftermath of José's murder and to face my emotions one last time.

I began a journal soon after the murder. It includes my thoughts about sadness, grief, and later some triumphs. I

can affirm how important it is to journal for persons who
are grieving.

I assure you that you as a victim, can rise from the
ashes. The journey will take time and seem endless, but
during the journey you will grow in unexpected ways. If
you persevere and give it your best shot, you might be
amazed at the good changes that happen.

It's still true that anger and fear often consume me. I
sometimes blurt out what I'm thinking when I feel I've
been wronged. I get very angry and always bring to task
those who hurt me. I do it without fear and with little
regard for embarrassment.

In 1996, I had an important end-of-year paper due in a
college class. The professor hadn't given the best of
instructions on what he wanted in the final paper. Some
students understood. I did not.

The professor gave a B minus when students didn't
understand, regardless of the strength of the essay.

I thought that was unjust and I blurted out in front of
the class, "That is ridiculous. You were not detailed
enough in your instructions!"

I continued on about how hard I had worked on my
project and received only a B minus.

The professor looked at me, sort of stammered, and
kept on speaking to the class.

I felt that I had spoken with disrespect, but I was right,
as several students told me later.

José's death taught me not to be obsessed with little
problems. But most importantly, I learned the value of
doing my best for my future.

I'm sure José would smile to know I've loved him for
more than fifty years. He lives in my heart, my memory,

and is a part of our family dynamics: he is often part of continuous stories shared with my children or my friends who knew him.

I think of him every day and that is as it should be. My life has soared and I haven't been stuck in endless grief. I have lived on with gusto.

I have traveled to Europe, Tibet, China, and Central America. I've seen most of the United States, including Alaska and Hawaii.

And I'm still learning. Currently, I'm studying to be an acrylic painter.

José left a wonderful legacy. Soon after his death, I attended memorial services in his honor.

By March 4, 1993, a makeshift cross was erected on the exit ramp where the murder happened.

As I recall, the cross was initiated by Veterans of Vietnam. It was a simple white cross and various citizens would stop and place flowers or notes in remembrance of José.

The cross has been refurbished several times in the years that have passed, and it might still be at that exit ramp where he died.

October 16, 1993, I participated in a wreath dedication at the National Law Enforcement Officer Memorial near Judiciary Square in Washington DC. The wreath was in honor of all fallen officers.

At that date, there were 13,256 names on the memorial wall. Many more have been added since.

Jennifer Filer, wife of Mark Filer who was killed in August 1993, accompanied me to lay the wreath.

In May 1994, my son and I attended a ceremony for the dedication of José's name being added on that National

Law Enforcement Memorial's Wall of the Fallen.

On February 25, 1998, my sister, brother-in-law, mother, and I attended the dedication of the Jose M Cavazos Memorial Bridge in Prince William County, Virginia. Marked with a large, green sign, it is at the Dale Boulevard overpass at Interstate 95, close to where José was killed.

I'm proud of my two intelligent adult children for their successes. I thank my daughter and son for the encouragement they provide me, for their love, and for the many times they answer my phone calls.

José and I have four granddaughters. They each are special and beautiful.

At the birth of each new baby grandchild, I have missed José. It is sad that their grandfather never shared their lives.

My life continues to transform, as does everyone's. It is in constant motion and I don't like to waste time.

I don't think I have learned every lesson yet. There are vacant places that I wish I could fill. But I try and think about my achievements instead of missing pieces.

There was an emptiness in my heart that I have tried very diligently to mend, but it hasn't disappeared. I know and am sure that José's life and memory are treasures that will always be with me. The emptiness is full of those memories.

It is difficult for me to explain, as I write these words years later, how debilitated I was by his death. I learned that pain diminishes with time, but never leaves completely. The good memories endure and help me remember José.

My entire world was shattered in the blink of an eye

one dark morning many years ago. But like many other survivors, I've rebounded and found unique paths to joy.

It is a journey I embrace with pride.

About the Author

Linda Queen Cavazos in Scotland

Linda is an artist who likes to travel and spend time with her grandchildren.